This book is provided to you as part of the Bookworm
program. When you are finished with it,

Pass It On

to someone who needs a book. Together, we can
build a community of readers.

Huntington City-Township
Public Library

255 W Park Dr, Huntington, IN 46750
155 W Sparks St, Markle, IN 46770

MAKE YOUR OWN

SCI-FI FLICK

by Jonathan Quijano

Consultant:
Tad Kershner
Founder
Montalto Visual

CAPSTONE PRESS
a capstone imprint

Velocity is published by Capstone Press,
1710 Roe Crest Drive, North Mankato, Minnesota 56003.
www.capstonepub.com

Books published by Capstone Press are manufactured with paper
containing at least 10 percent post-consumer waste.

Library of Congress Cataloging-in-Publication Data
Quijano, Jonathan.
Make your own sci-fi flick / by Jonathan Quijano.
  p. cm. -- (Velocity: make your movie)
Summary: "Provides instructions for how to make your own science fiction
movie"--Provided by publisher.
Includes bibliographical references and index.
Includes webliography.
ISBN 978-1-4296-7531-4 (library binding)
1. Science fiction films--Production and direction--Juvenile literature.
I. Title. II. Series.

PN1995.9.S26Q55 2012
791.43'615--dc23
2011029188

Editorial Credits

Editor: Lisa Owings
Designer: Emily Love

Media Researcher: Anastasia Scott
Editorial Director: Patricia Stockland

Photo Credits
Quavondo/iStockphoto, cover (foreground); Zmeel Photography/iStockphoto, cover (background);
NASA, ESA, and the Hubble Heritage (STScI/AURA)-ESA/Hubble Collaboration, cover (background),
34; Twentieth Century Fox Film Corporation/Everett Collection, 4, 5, 6, 8 (top), 9 (top, bottom),
20 (bottom), 25 (top, bottom); Mary Evans/AMBLIN/Ronald Grant/Everett Collection, 7 (top);
Kovalenko Iurii/Bigstock, 7 (middle); Mary Evans/Ronald Grant/Everett Collection, 7 (bottom); Everett
Collection, 8 (bottom), 33; Fotolia, 10 (top); Roxana Gonzalez/Bigstock, 10 (bottom); Andrea Danti/
Bigstock, 11, 30; Jon Quijano/Red Line Editorial, 12; Rick Orndorf, 14, 21, 26, 27 (top, middle,
bottom), 28 (top, bottom), 29, 30 (top), 31, 37, 44; Mary Evans/Henson Associates /ITC/Universal
Pictures/Ronald Grant/Everett Collection, 15; Red Line Editorial, 16, 17, 24, 41; Janus Films/
Photofest, 18; Martin Garnham/Shutterstock Images, 19 (top); Alexey Stiop/Shutterstock Images, 19
(bottom); Tono Balaguer/Bigstock, 20 (top); Paramount/Everett Collection, 22 (top); Darren Mower/
iStockphoto, 22 (bottom); Focus Features/Everett Collection, 23; Mary Evans/Paramount Pictures/
Ronald Grant/Everett Collection, 30 (bottom), 38–39; Bigstock, 32; Piotr Marcinski/Bigstock, 36
(person); Romulus Hossu/Dreamstime, 36 (object); Bill Casey/Bigstock, 40; Igor Terekhov/Bigstock, 42
(bottom); Steve Cukrov/Bigstock, 42 (top); Shutterstock Images, 45

Printed in the United States of America in Stevens Point, Wisconsin.
102011   006404WZS12

TABLE OF CONTENTS

Introduction to SCIENCE FICTION FILMS

Have you ever dreamed of living in a world completely different from your own? Now is your chance to create and explore that world by making your own sci-fi flick.

Science fiction is a popular movie **genre**. Audiences watch sci-fi movies to experience unfamiliar places, characters, and events. Strange planets, alien spaceships, time travel, and advanced technology are all part of the world of sci-fi.

genre—a category of art characterized by similarities in form, style, or subject matter

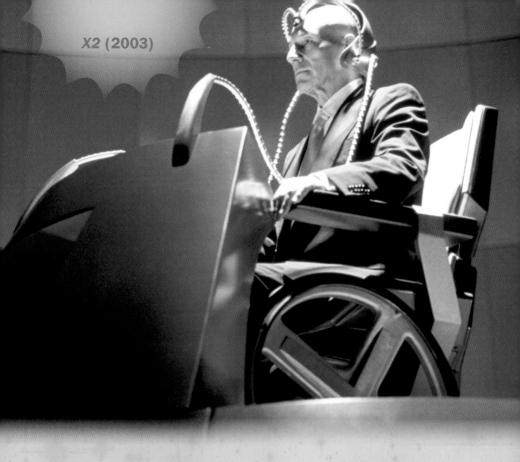

WHAT IS SCIENCE FICTION?

Science fiction is about imaginary events that have a scientific explanation. The scientific explanation doesn't have to make sense in our world. But it should make sense in your sci-fi world. For example, humans cannot move objects with their minds. However, your movie might invent a scientific reason why a character has this ability.

WHAT IF?

Ideas for a great sci-fi movie often begin with the question, "What if?" A filmmaker might ask, "What if people traveled to the center of the sun?" or "What if computers were as smart as humans?" Ask yourself "What if?" and see where it leads you.

5

SCI-FI FEATURES

TECHNOLOGY

Almost all sci-fi movies are based on technology. Technology can tell your audience a lot about your sci-fi world. It can tell them how advanced a society is. It can also tell them if a society often engages in battle with others.

THE FUTURE

Many sci-fi movies are set in the future. Making movies about the future lets filmmakers use their creativity. The future can be anything they imagine.

Roland Emmerich's
The Day After Tomorrow (2004)

TIME TRAVEL

What would happen if a time machine allowed you to travel to the past or future? Many sci-fi movies try to answer this question.

Robert Zemeckis'
***Back to the Future* (1985)**

SPACE TRAVEL

Sci-fi movies are often set in a time when space travel is a normal part of life. Audiences get to feel the wonder of space travel.

ALIENS

Movies about aliens explore the idea that we are not alone in the universe. Some sci-fi movies are about humans meeting aliens on other planets. Others are about aliens visiting Earth.

Jonathan Frakes'
***Star Trek: First Contact* (1996)**

POPULAR SCI-FI MOVIES

Star Wars (1977–2005)

This classic sci-fi series is a space adventure set "a long time ago in a galaxy far, far away."

Features: technology, space travel, aliens

E.T.: The Extra-Terrestrial (1982)

E.T. is a friendly alien stranded on Earth. Ten-year-old Elliott develops a special connection with E.T.

Features: space travel, aliens

Back to the Future (1985)

A teenager accidentally travels back in time. He meets his parents when they were in high school.

Features: technology, time travel

Minority Report (2002)

Decades in the future, crimes can be predicted before they happen. The police arrest people before they do anything wrong.

Features: technology, the future

Avatar (2009)

Scientists study aliens called the Na'vi who live on a moon called Pandora. Humans want to mine a valuable mineral found on Pandora.

Features: technology, aliens

Creating Your Story

Every sci-fi movie starts with an imaginative story. Try the following to come up with ideas.

- Watch other sci-fi movies or read sci-fi novels.

- Think about what would happen if future scientists discovered how to do something that is impossible now. How would this affect people's lives?

- Read a science or technology magazine such as *Popular Science* or *Technology Review*. These magazines feature new inventions. Imagine how advanced the inventions will be in 1,000 years.

- Imagine what it would be like to visit a time and place in the distant past or future.

- Imagine what home and school life will be like for a kid 200 years from now.

Three-Act Structure

Like all good stories, sci-fi stories need three main parts: a beginning, a middle, and an end. In movies and plays, these parts are called acts.

ACT 1

- Something unexpected happens or a conflict breaks out in the sci-fi world. *For example, a large asteroid is about to smash into Earth.*

- The main character decides how to fix the problem. *A brave astronaut decides to travel to the asteroid. She plans to use the jets of the spaceship to push the asteroid on a new path.*

ACT 2

- The main character meets obstacles. The problem is more challenging than expected. *The astronaut's jets aren't strong enough to push the asteroid.*

- The main character discovers something that might fix the problem. *The jets can be used to push a smaller asteroid into the large asteroid. This would push it out of Earth's path.*

ACT 3

- The story reaches its **climax** when the main character puts his or her plan to the test. *Will the new plan to push the asteroid work, or will Earth be destroyed?*

- The main character either succeeds or fails. It's up to you!

climax—the most exciting or important part of a story

Writing Your Script

```
EXT. ON TOP OF A DESERTED HILL — DAY

PHILIP CHARMA walks slowly up a grassy hill. The wind
swirls. MOTHMA GREEBO, an alien creature wearing a long
blue robe, stands at the top of the hill.

Philip sees Mothma and waves his hand. They stand a few
yards apart.

                    MOTHMA
               (in the Egushu alien language)
          Greetings, stranger.

                    PHILIP
          I am a human from planet Earth. I do not speak
          your language. My ship crashed on your planet. I
          can't get home.

                    MOTHMA
               (in English)
          Then you have come to the right person.

Philip looks at Mothma in surprise.

                    PHILIP
               (cautiously)
          How do you know my language?
```

Once you know your story, you can write your **script**. It contains all the **dialogue** and action that takes place in your movie.

Before you start writing, think about how long you want your sci-fi flick to be. A film industry rule of thumb is that one page of the script will equal about one minute of screen time. Follow the standard format shown above. Use Courier 12-point font. As you write, remember that a 30-minute movie can be just as exciting as a 90-minute film.

HEADINGS

- Start each scene with a heading that includes the place and time in which the scene is set. Use *INT.* (interior) or *EXT.* (exterior) to show whether the scene takes place indoors or outside. Use *DAY* for daytime scenes and *NIGHT* for evening and nighttime scenes. Make a new heading each time you move to a different place.

DESCRIPTION

- Describe the action throughout the scene. What are the characters doing?
- Describe the sights and sounds in each scene. What are the characters seeing, hearing, and reacting to?

DIALOGUE

- Write the speaker's name in capital letters centered above each character's line.
- Write your characters' dialogue. It is usually best to let your actors decide how to deliver their lines. However, you can include instructions in parentheses if needed.
- If a character speaks in an alien language, write the alien character's lines in English. Note in parentheses what language the character is speaking.

script—the written text of a movie

dialogue—a conversation between two or more characters

BREAKING DOWN YOUR SCRIPT

Most movies are shot out of order. All scenes that take place in the same location are shot at once. To stay organized, do what professional filmmakers do and break down your script. Go through your completed script. Make a list of where and when each scene needs to be shot. Also list the characters and props present in each scene. Group together all scenes that need to be shot in the same place and time of day. Use your list to make a schedule for your shoot. If you need to shoot outside, have a backup plan in case of bad weather.

Finding Cast and Crew

As the director of a sci-fi flick, you will need to find a cast to bring your sci-fi world to life. You will also need a crew to help you behind the scenes. Ask your friends and relatives if they would like to help you with your movie.

You can also ask your classmates or hold auditions at school. You could even play a few roles yourself!

TIP

Younger kids in costumes can play strange creatures or tiny aliens.

① The mystic valley — Jens small figure is visible, slow zoom in to Jen. Over the mountains a storm approaches.

② cut to Jen playing strange 2 pronged flute

STORYBOARDING

Sci-fi scenes require a lot of planning. Most special effects are added after the shoot. You must know where the special-effect shots will fit before you start shooting.

Storyboarding is important because shooting sci-fi scenes is complex. Storyboard your sci-fi scenes by making a sketch of each planned shot. This will help you remember what shots and special effects you need.

BUILD A SET

Building a set takes time and effort. However, a set is useful if you plan to shoot many scenes in that location. Here are some ways to make a spaceship set look realistic:

WALL CONTROL PANEL

You will need:

- empty bookshelf
- scissors
- colored vellum paper
- nearby electrical outlet
- small lamps
- tape
- dark gray construction paper, long and wide enough to cover the front of the shelf

1. Cut holes in the construction paper.

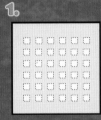

2. Tape colored vellum paper to the back of the construction paper, behind the holes.

3. Place small lamps on the empty bookshelf. Tape the lamp cords together. Plug the lamps into the outlet.

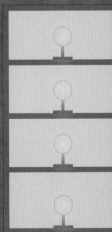

4. Tape the construction paper over the front of the bookshelf. The lamps will light the colored buttons and shapes from behind.

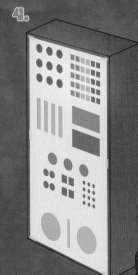

NAVIGATION DESK

You will need:

colored vellum paper

heavy dark gray construction paper

large piece of corrugated cardboard, painted dark gray

tape

small lamps

nearby electrical outlet

scissors

4 heavy cardboard tubes about 3 feet (0.9 meters) long, painted dark gray

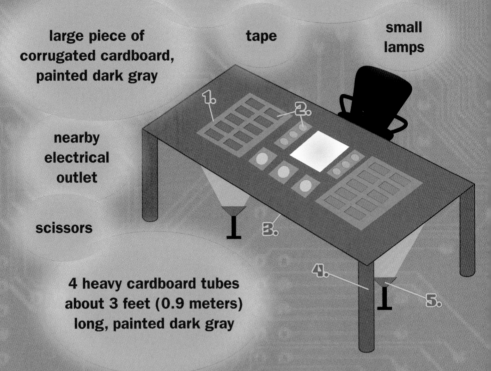

1. Cut holes in the cardboard. These will be the spaces for your control panels.

2. Following steps 1 and 2 on page 16, make control panels to fit the holes in the cardboard.

3. Tape the control panels to the back of the cardboard, behind the matching holes.

4. Attach a cardboard tube under each corner of the desk with tape. These will be the legs the desk stands on.

5. Light the desk from beneath with lamps. To hide the lamps from view, you can attach a second piece of cardboard to the front of the desk. You can also frame your shots to show only the top of the desk.

Find Futuristic Locations

Alphaville **(1965)** is an old movie that teaches an important lesson. The *Alphaville* filmmakers created a futuristic look without building a set. They shot in buildings with unique architecture, automatic doors, and other modern elements.

Use *Alphaville*'s strategy for your film. Look for modern and unusual buildings in your area. Be sure to ask permission before filming in any location.

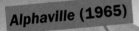

Alphaville (1965)

Possible locations:

· libraries, art museums, homes, and office buildings with modern architecture

· public parking ramps

· new shopping malls

Rehearse the scene until everything runs smoothly before shooting in public. Your shooting time in a public location may be limited. Rehearsal will help reduce mistakes and

Mixing Locations

It can be hard to find a building with both an interior and exterior that works for your scene. Mixing locations is a good solution. You can film your exterior shots outside one building. Then you can film your interior shots in a different building.

Let's say your characters encounter a blip in the space-time continuum. Your first shots could be taken outside a very modern-looking building, such as an art museum. Your next shots would film your actors entering the museum. The rest of your scene could be filmed inside an old courthouse, library, or other historic location. When the characters come through the doors, they act amazed to suddenly find themselves in a very old-fashioned place. When edited together, your scene looks like it happens all in one location.

COSTUMES, MAKEUP, AND PROPS

The right costumes, makeup, and props let the audience know your movie is set in a different time or place.

SCI-FI WARDROBE

Featureless clothing with clean lines makes actors look like they belong in a futuristic world.

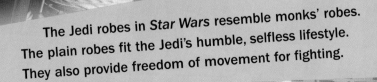

The Jedi robes in *Star Wars* resemble monks' robes. The plain robes fit the Jedi's humble, selfless lifestyle. They also provide freedom of movement for fighting.

A white protective suit, white gloves, and white boots can make a convincing space suit. Old snowmobile or motorcycle helmets make good space helmets. Hide the brand name with tape that matches the color of the helmet.

CREATE AN ALIEN WITH MAKEUP

Actors often play aliens in sci-fi films. You can use makeup to transform your actors into aliens.

THE ALIEN WITH SUBTLE DIFFERENCES

Star Trek's Spock
Star Trek II: The Wrath of Khan **(1982)**

- **Pointy ears:** Attach prostheses with spirit gum. Use concealer to blend prostheses with skin. (Prostheses and spirit gum are available in costume shops.)

- **Slanted eyebrows:** Use concealer to hide the outer half of brows. Use a grease pen, brow pencil, or eyeliner to draw brows that slant up.

Optional: Finish the look with a Vulcan wig (available at costume shops).

THE ALIEN WITH OBVIOUS DIFFERENCES

- **Reptile makeup:** Use green, yellow, and blue face paint to paint a section of the actor's face and neck. Be sure to cover all areas of the skin, including the ears.

- **Shedding skin:** Apply flesh-colored liquid latex overlapping the edges of the painted area. Use concealer to blend the liquid latex into the surrounding skin. When the latex is dry, peel the edges back.

TIP Try applying different colors and patterns of face paint to create your own alien look.

22

One Sci-Fi Prop

Eternal Sunshine of the Spotless Mind (2004) is set in the present time. The characters have regular homes, jobs, and clothes. A single sci-fi prop helps transform this movie into a gripping science fiction film. It is the machine used to erase the main character's memories of his ex-girlfriend.

Search for items to base your movie on. Look for props at thrift stores, garage sales, or at home. A modified skateboard could serve as a time travel device. Use a TV remote to serve as a mind-control device. Each object has many sci-fi possibilities!

prosthesis—an artificial device that replaces or enhances a body part

ACT 2:
Lights, Camera, Action!

Lighting

Classic Hollywood lighting uses three lights. Three-point lighting produces bright, even light. The audience can see every detail in the scene.

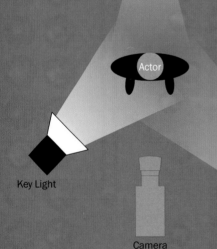

3. The Back Light

The back light shines from behind your subject. It helps set your actor apart from the background.

2. The Fill Light

The fill light is a secondary light. It lightens the shadows created by the key light.

1. The Key Light

The key light is the main light on your subject. It is the brightest light, and it casts the darkest shadows.

TIP

You can use the lamps in your home as movie lights. Put the same kind of light bulb in every lamp.

Back Light

Actor

Key Light

Camera

Fill Light

24

Dramatic Lighting

- Bright three-point lighting is good for early scenes with less excitement. But as the drama increases, the lighting should get more dramatic too. Create drama by removing lights to cast shadows.

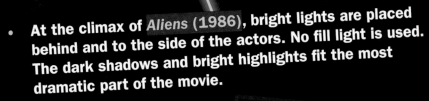

- At the climax of Aliens (1986), bright lights are placed behind and to the side of the actors. No fill light is used. The dark shadows and bright highlights fit the most dramatic part of the movie.

- Only a back light is used in this shot. It enhances the robot's dramatic entrance.

Finding a Camera

You can use almost any type of camera to shoot your sci-fi flick. See if a friend or family member will lend you a video camera. Higher-quality cameras are available for rent. With a bit of creativity, even the video function on your point-and-shoot camera or cell phone would work.

Shoot for Editing

Film each scene multiple times from different perspectives. That way you will have plenty of options for editing the scene. Film at least the following shots:

ESTABLISHING SHOT

An establishing shot shows where the scene takes place. Use it at the beginning of a scene.

MASTER SHOT

A master shot shows all of the actors performing the entire scene. The master shot is the foundation of your scene. Cut away from the master shot to show details.

MEDIUM SHOTS AND CLOSE-UPS

Get a variety of shots of all your actors during each scene. A close-up brings special attention to a specific detail in a scene.

Medium Shot (MS): shows the actor from above the knee

Close-Up (CU): shows the actor's head and shoulders

Extreme Close-Up (XCU): shows only the actor's face or part of the face

cut—to change from one shot to another

Reaction Shots

Show each actor's response to other actors or events.

Insert Shots

Get close-ups of important details in a scene, such as a flashing control panel or a crack in the spaceship. Insert shots often focus on an object that will become important later on. For example, a dangling microphone could show that a crew member has abandoned her post. This could set up a suspenseful moment later as a message sent to her gets no response.

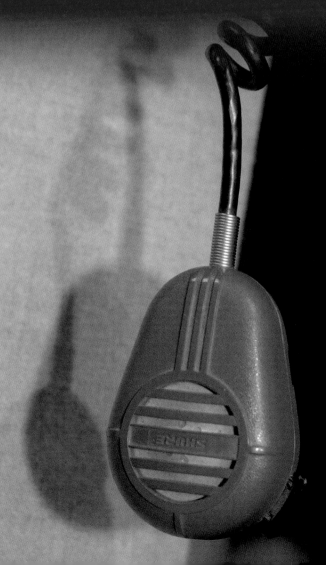

Directing a Sci-Fi Space Battle

Star Trek II: The Wrath of Khan includes a battle between the Starship *Enterprise* and the Starship *Reliant*. The scene has cool shots of the ships firing at each other. But most of the scene shows the crew in the *Enterprise* control room.

Directing these battle scenes required good communication. No shots of the spaceships existed yet. The director had to explain how the shots of the crew would fit in with shots of the ships.

To direct a similar battle scene, you need to:

1. Use storyboarding to plan the shots you need.

2. Explain to the actors how you picture the complete battle scene. Let the actors know how their shots will fit in.

3. Film all the speaking parts.

4. Film all the physical action. For example, maybe your ship takes a hit during the battle. Film a shot of the crew being thrown to the ground.

5. During editing, arrange the shots of the crew to match up with the shots of the battling ships.

TIP If you do a shot in which actors need to fall to the ground, be safe. Set down cushions for the actors to land on when they fall. Zoom in so the cushions are not in the shot.

ACT 3:
SPECIAL EFFECTS

Science fiction is known for its use of special effects. There are two kinds of special effects. Practical special effects are filmed live. Filming a model spaceship to make it look real is a practical special effect.

Computer-generated imagery (CGI) does not need to be filmed. You use video editing software to add these special effects after filming. Using computer effects to make it look like a spaceship is firing lasers is an example of CGI.

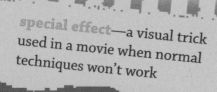

special effect—a visual trick used in a movie when normal techniques won't work

Chroma-Keying

Chroma-keying allows you to set a scene in a place you can't film in, such as the surface of the moon. First, you film your scene in front of a green background called a green screen. Later, you use video editing software to replace the green background with one that fits the scene.

Look for otherworldly stock backgrounds online, or buy software that includes a variety of backgrounds. You can also film your own backgrounds.

Andy and Lana Wachowski's *The Matrix* (1999)

TIP

Nothing you want in your green screen shot can be green. Chroma-keying will remove it along with the background. Remember this no-green rule when choosing costumes!

How to Chroma-Key

1. Choose or film your background.

2. Draw storyboards showing where the actors will stand against the background. Use these storyboards to position your actors in the shot.

3. Film scenes with your actors in front of a green screen. Actors should stand far enough from the screen so that they don't cast shadows on it. Light the scene evenly to get rid of any shadows. Shadows make chroma-keying difficult.

4. Remove the green background from your scene. Most editing software has an option for this.

5. Replace the green background with the new background.

Tip

The light needs to come from the same direction in both the background and green screen shots. Mismatched lighting will ruin the illusion.

MAKE YOUR OWN GREEN SCREEN

You will need:

thumbtacks
or tape

an 8- by 12-foot (2.4- by 3.7-meter)
section of bright green,
nonreflective fabric

1. Iron your fabric if it is wrinkled or creased.

2. Use thumbtacks or tape to hang your green screen on a wall.

Optional: If you have more money to spend, you can buy special green screen material or a premade green screen. These are available online.

TIP Backgrounds with distant objects work well for chroma-keying. It's harder to tell that the backgrounds were added into the shots.

Use the Force

Create the illusion that characters can move objects with their minds.

1. Film the actor throwing an object to the floor.

2. Use your editing program to play the shot in reverse. Now it looks like the object is flying into your actor's hand!

TIP Film this shot a few times. Get a close-up of the object leaving the actor's hand. Also get a close-up of the object landing on the floor. Mix the close-ups with the master shot to sell the effect.

Beam Me Up!

Teleporters are high-tech sci-fi transportation devices. How nice would it be to just "beam" from one place to another? Here's how to create the teleporting effect:

1. Place the camera on a tripod to keep it still.

2. Film your actor standing in the scene for about 15 seconds.

3. Have the actor leave the set. Film the background for about 15 seconds.

4. In editing, **dissolve** from the first shot to the second shot. Your actor will seem to disappear.

   Optional: Download a digital animation of shimmering light to place over the actor as he or she disappears.

5. Add a sound effect for the transporter. Try making one yourself. The sound could be as simple as playing a chord on an electronic keyboard.

dissolve—to gradually transition from one shot to another

Miniatures

Sci-fi filmmakers are masters of illusion. They often use miniature objects or sets. They film them straight on or from a low angle instead of from above. This makes the miniatures look life-size.

Star Trek III: The Search for Spock (1984)

MAKE MODEL SPACESHIPS LOOK REAL

Model and hobby shops will have models of spaceships, cars, and other vehicles. You can buy a model already put together or build one from a kit. You can also use what you find to make an original creation. Many filmmakers mix and match parts from different model kits to make something new.

Hang model spaceships against a background of black fabric. Use black thread to hang the ships. The thread will be invisible against the black background. Move your camera around the ships as you film. This makes the ships look like they are moving.

TIP

You can also film your model spaceships against a green screen. Use green thread to hang the ships. Then replace the background with deep space scenery.

Well done! You are finished filming and creating special effects! Now it's time to edit your footage to create a finished movie.

Editing

Editing is the process of taking the best footage you shot and building it into finished scenes. Most computers come with basic video editing software. Use the software to cut your video clips into smaller sections. Then arrange the clips in **sequences**. You can also add special effects during editing. Check your software's manual or help function to learn how to add laser blasts, wormholes, starry skies, alien landscapes, and much more.

MAKE A MONTAGE

Montages are handy in sci-fi movies. Many things in sci-fi movies take a long time. Traveling to another planet, learning about an alien race, or developing new technology might take years in your movie. A montage can show these things happening quickly, saving room for other scenes. Make a montage using a simple editing technique called a dissolve. Dissolves create transitions between the scenes in your montage. These transitions help show the passage of time.

TIP

Select shots with little dialogue for your montage. Add background music in place of dialogue to accompany your action shots.

Create a Dissolve

1. Place two clips next to each other in your editing program.

2. Drag the second clip back to slightly overlap the end of the first clip. Your editing program should automatically dissolve between these shots. If not, add a dissolve transition.

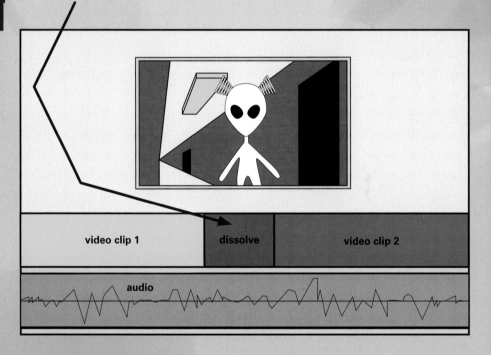

| video clip 1 | dissolve | video clip 2 |

audio

sequence—a series of shots

montage—a series of shots that shows a lot of time passing quickly by focusing on a few important moments

Sci-Fi Sound

Most sound effects are added to the movie during editing. These sound effects are called Foley. It's fun to record your own sci-fi Foley. Here are some ideas for sound effects:

Robot Moving

garage door opening; electric drill whirring

Ship's Door Opening

air rushing out of a soda bottle

Alien Language

clips of the actor reading different foreign languages, edited together and played at a slow speed

Spaceship Engines Rumbling

bowling ball rolling

Transporter Beam

keyboard chord

TIP

You can download or purchase premade sound effects. Most editing software also includes sound effects.

THE SCORE

Once you're finished editing your footage, it's time to create a score. A good sci-fi score needs to reflect the kind of movie you are making. If your movie is about exploring space, the score could be soft and eerie. If your movie has a bunch of space battles, you should have a pounding, aggressive score.

How to Make Your Score

♪ Use existing music. Classical music is a good resource. It is easy to find and covers a wide range of moods. Look online for royalty-free music, which you can use without paying fees.

♪ Ask a musically talented friend or family member to write and record music for your film.

♪ If you have musical training, try writing the score yourself. Watch your edited film and decide where to put music. Time how long the music needs to last in each spot. Write and record music to fit these spaces.

Use your editing software to add your score. Now your movie is complete! It takes just a few minutes to burn your movie to DVD after you save your file.

Gustav Holst's
The Planets

The Planets is an orchestral suite, performed for the first time in 1918. The suite has seven sections. Composer Gustav Holst wrote each section to represent a different planet in the solar system: Mercury, Venus, Mars, Jupiter, Saturn, Uranus, and Neptune.

The Planets forever influenced sci-fi music. The angry-sounding music that represented Mars was the model for the villain's theme in *Star Wars*. See if *The Planets* inspires your own sci-fi score!

score—the music accompanying a movie

EPILOGUE:
YOUR PREMIERE

Now that you've completed your sci-fi flick, you can show your movie to the world! First, you need a place to screen your movie.

The Safe Bet: Screen it at home.

- Play the movie on the biggest screen in the biggest room in your house.

Extra Credit: Find a public place to screen your movie.

- Small, local movie theaters often rent out their screens.
- A local school or library might let you reserve a projection room.

Give Your Premiere a Sci-Fi Theme

- Send out invitations in advance. Decorate the invitations with a few dramatic images from your movie.

- Ask your guests to dress in costumes that fit your movie's theme.

- Serve sci-fi themed food and beverages. If your movie is about space travel, you could decorate **star-shaped cookies with silver sprinkles**. If the characters in your movie eat only liquid food, serve smoothies or milkshakes.

- Use props or objects from your set as decorations.

- Play music from your score in the background.

GLOSSARY

climax (KLYE-maks)—the most exciting or important part of a story

cut (KUHT)—to change from one shot to another

dialogue (DYE-uh-lawg)—a conversation between two or more characters

dissolve (di-ZAHLV)—to gradually transition from one shot to another

genre (ZHAHN-ruh)—a category of art characterized by similarities in form, style, or subject matter

montage (MAHN-tahj)—a series of shots that shows a lot of time passing quickly by focusing on a few important moments

prosthesis (prahs-THEE-sis)—an artificial device that replaces or enhances a body part

score (SKOR)—the music accompanying a movie

script (SKRIPT)—the written text of a movie

sequence (SEE-kwuhns)—a series of shots

special effect (SPESH-uhl i-FEKT)—a visual trick used in a movie when normal techniques won't work

READ MORE

Grabham, Tim. *Movie Maker*. Somerville, Mass.: Candlewick Press, 2010.

Lanier, Troy, and Clay Nichols. *Filmmaking for Teens: Pulling Off Your Shorts*. Studio City, Calif.: Michael Weise Productions, 2010.

Miles, Liz. *Movie Special Effects*. Culture in Action. Chicago: Raintree, 2010.

Throp, Claire. *Exploring Other Worlds: What Is Science Fiction?* Culture in Action. Chicago: Raintree, 2010.

INTERNET SITES

FactHound offers a safe, fun way to find Internet sites related to this book. All of the sites on FactHound have been researched by our staff.

Here's all you do:

Visit *www.facthound.com*

Type in this code: 9781429675314

INDEX

aliens, 4, 7, 8, 9, 12–13, 14, 22, 42

cameras, 25
camera shots, 26–29
casting, 14
chroma-keying, 33–35, 39
climax, 11, 25
costumes, 14, 20–21, 33, 45

dialogue, 12–13, 41
directing, 14, 30–31

editing, 19, 26, 31, 32, 33, 34, 36, 37, 40–41, 42–43

filming, 18–19, 26–29, 31, 32, 33–35, 36–39, 40
filming locations, 14, 16, 18–19
Foley, 37, 42
future, the, 6–7, 9, 10, 18, 20

green screens. *See* chroma-keying

lighting, 24–25, 34

makeup, 20, 22
miniatures, 38–39

premieres, 44–45
props, 14, 20, 23, 45

rehearsals, 18

scores, 43, 45
scripts, 12–13, 14
sets, 16–17, 18, 37, 38, 45
sound effects. *See* Foley
spaceships, 4, 11, 16–17, 29, 30–31, 32, 38–39, 42, 45
space travel, 7, 8, 9, 45
special effects, 15, 32–39, 40
story, 10–11
storyboarding, 15, 31, 34

technology, 4, 6, 8, 9, 10, 40
three-act structure, 11
time travel, 4, 7, 8, 19, 23